REDOUTÉ'S
FABULOUS FLOWERS

REDOUTÉ'S
FABULOUS FLOWERS

PIERRE-JOSEPH REDOUTÉ

DOVER PUBLICATIONS
GARDEN CITY, NEW YORK

Bibliographical Note

Redouté's Fabulous Flowers is a new work, first published by Dover Publications in 2019. The plates are reproduced from standard editions of Redouté's collections.

Library of Congress Cataloging-in-Publication Data

Names: Redouté, Pierre Joseph, 1759–1840, artist.
Title: Redouté's fabulous flowers / Pierre-Joseph Redouté.
Description: Garden City, New York : Dover Publications 2019. | "Redouté's
   Fabulous Flowers is a new work, first published by Dover Publications in 2019.
   The plates are from standard editions of Redouté's collections."
Identifiers: LCCN 2018039869 | ISBN 9780486827780 (paperback) |
   ISBN 048682778X (paperback)
Subjects: LCSH: Redouté, Pierre Joseph, 1759–1840 Themes, motives. |
   Flowers in art. | BISAC: ART / European. | NATURE / Plants / Flowers.
Classification: LCC QK98.183.R43 A2 2019 | DDC 581.7—dc23
LC record available at https://lccn.loc.gov/2018039869

Manufactured in the United States by LSC Communications Book LLC
82778X02   2021
www.doverpublications.com

NOTE

Pierre-Joseph Redouté (1759–1840) is one of the most accomplished botanical painters, known especially for his depictions of roses and lilies. In his lifetime, he was called the Raphael of Flowers. He is to flower paintings what John James Audubon is to bird paintings. Redouté created more than 2,100 paintings featuring more than 1,800 species.

Redouté was born in the Netherlands (in present-day Belgium) and lived most of his life in France. He tutored Marie Antoinette, the last Queen of France, and was named Draughtsman and Painter to the Queen's Cabinet. Empress Josephine, the first wife of Napoleon Bonaparte, was his patron and had him paint flowers in the garden at their estate. Louise of Orléans, the Queen of Belgium, was also his pupil. Redouté received the Legion of Honor medal in France and was knighted in Belgium.

He found favor with powerful admirers, across borders and despite political upheaval. His meticulously accurate watercolors impressed botanists as well as fine art aficionados. Today his botanical prints are beloved in framed pictures, books, and china patterns.

Flowers are the epitome of natural beauty. Redouté captured, celebrated, and championed their beauty, drawing attention to many varieties of flowers that would otherwise go unappreciated. Captions include the English common name and the Latin species name for eighty different types of flowers.

LIST OF PLATES

REDOUTÉ'S
FABULOUS FLOWERS

PLATE 1

ALPINE ROSE WITH GLOBOSE RECEPTACLE AND GLABROUS PEDICEL

(*Rosa alpina laevis*)

PLATE 2
AMARYLLIS
(*Amaryllis regnae*)

PLATE 3

ANEMONE

(*Anemone coronaria*)

PLATE 4
ANJOU ROSE
(*Rosa andegavensis*)

PLATE 5

AUSTRIAN COPPER (CORN POPPY ROSE)

(Rosa eglanteria punicea)

PLATE 6
BARBADOS LILY
(*Amaryllis equestris*)

PLATE 7

BISHOP ROSE

(Rosa gallica purpurea-violacea magna)

PLATE 8
BLUE PLANTAIN LILY
(*Hemerocallis coerulea*)

PLATE 9
BLUISH-LEAVED PROVINS ROSE
(Rosa gallica caerulea)

PLATE 10

BURNET ROSE

(*Rosa pimpinelli marioeburgensis*)

PLATE 11
CABBAGE ROSE
(*Rosa centifolia*)

PLATE 12
CANADIAN LILY
(*Lilium penduliflorum*)

PLATE 13
CANARY ISLANDS HIBISCUS
(*Lavatera phoenicea*)

PLATE 14
CANARY YELLOW ROSE
(*Rosa eglanteria luteola*)

PLATE 17
CHILD OF FRANCE
(*Rosa gallica agatha delphiniana*)

PLATE 19
COMMON HYACINTH
(*Hyacinthus orientalis linnaeus*)

PLATE 20
CORYMBOSE CAROLINA ROSE
(*Rosa carolina corymbosa*)

PLATE 21
CROWN IMPERIAL
(*Fritillaria imperialis*)

PLATE 22
CULTIVATED BANANA
(*Musa paradisiaca*)

PLATE 24
DALMATIAN IRIS
(*Iris pallida*)

PLATE 25
DECUMBENT ALPINE ROSE
(*Rosa alpina debilis*)

PLATE 26
DIDIER'S TULIP
(*Tulipa gesneriana*)

PLATE 27

DUCHESS OF ORLEANS

(*Rosa gallica aurelianensis*)

PLATE 28
ENGLISH IRIS
(*Iris xyphioides*)

PLATE 29
FRANKFORT ROSE
(*Rosa turbinata*)

PLATE 31
GERMAN FLAG IRIS
(*Iris germanica*)

PLATE 32
GEUM
(*Geum chilense*)

PLATE 34
GLOSSY ROSE
(*Rosa lucida*)

PLATE 37
HIPPEASTRUM
(Hippeastrum puniceum)

PLATE 39

HYDRANGEA

(Hydrangea macrophylla)

PLATE 40
LADY'S SLIPPER ORCHID
(*Cypripedium calceolus*)

PLATE 41
LEADWORT
(*Plumbago auriculata*)

PLATE 42
L'HERITIER'S ROSE
(*Rosa lheritieranea*)

PLATE 43
MADONNA LILY
(*Lilium candidum*)

PLATE 44
MALMEDY ROSE
(*Rosa malmundariensis*)

PLATE 45
MEADOW SAFFRON
(*Colchicum autumnale*)

PLATE 46
OPIUM POPPY
(*Papaver somniferum*)

PLATE 48
PAINTED DAISY
(*Chrysanthemum carinatum*)

PLATE 49
PANSIES
(*Viola tricolor*)

PLATE 50
PINEAPPLE
(*Bromelia ananas*)

PLATE 51
PINK HEDGE ROSE
(*Rosa sepium rosea*)

PLATE 52
PORTLAND ROSE
(*Rosa damascena coccinea*)

PLATE 53
RED GIANT
(*Amaryllis vittata*)

PLATE 54
RED-HOT POKER
(*Tritoma uvaria*)

PLATE 55
RED-LEAVED ROSE
(*Rosa rubrifolia*)

PLATE 56
ROSA MUNDI (STRIPED ROSE OF FRANCE)
(*Rosa gallica versicolor*)

PLATE 57
ROSE OF LOVE
(*Rosa pumila*)

PLATE 58
ROSENBERG'S ROSE
(*Rosa rosenbergiana*)

PLATE 59

SEMI-DOUBLE MUSK ROSE

(*Rosa moschata flore semi-pleno*)

PLATE 60
SEMI-DOUBLE SWEETBRIAR
(*Rosa rubiginosa flore semi-pleno*)

PLATE 61
SHORT-STYLED ROSE WITH YELLOWISH WHITE FLOWERS
(Rosa bevistyla)

PLATE 62
SINGLE MAY ROSE
(*Rosa cinnamomea flore simplici*)

PLATE 63
SINGLE PROVINS ROSE
(*Rosa gallica rosea flore simplici*)

PLATE 64
SONG OF INDIA
(*Dracoena reflexa*)

PLATE 66
SPINY-LEAVED ROSE OF DEMETRA
(*Rosa spinulifolia dematriana*)

PLATE 67
ST. JAMES LILY
(*Amaryllis formosissima*)

PLATE 68
SWEETBRIAR ROSE
(*Rosa rubignosa cretica*)

PLATE 70
TIGER LILY
(*Lilium tigrinum*)

PLATE 71
TUBEROSE
(*Polianthes tuberosa*)

PLATE 73
TWIN-FLOWERED ROSE
(*Rosa geminata*)

PLATE 74

VAN EEDEN'S ROSE

(*Rosa gallica purpurea velutina parva*)

PLATE 75
VARIEGATED ALPINE ROSE
(*Rosa alpina flore variegato*)

PLATE 76
WALLFLOWER
(*Cheiranthus cheiri*)

PLATE 77
WHITE MOSS ROSE
(*Rosa muscosa alba*)

PLATE 78
WHITE-FLOWERED ROSE
(*Rosa leucantha*)

PLATE 79
YELLOW FLAG
(*Iris pseudacorus*)

PLATE 80
YELLOW MULTI-FLOWERED NARCISSUS
(*Narcissus lazetta*)